She was actually a Halloween witch, but she liked Christmas better.

It was almost Christmas.
And the witch was *so* excited.

Every year on Christmas Eve, she would stand by her front window. Hidden by her spider web curtains, she would watch the villagers celebrate in the small town square below.

They would sing, dance and laugh. They were so eager for the arrival of Santa Claus.

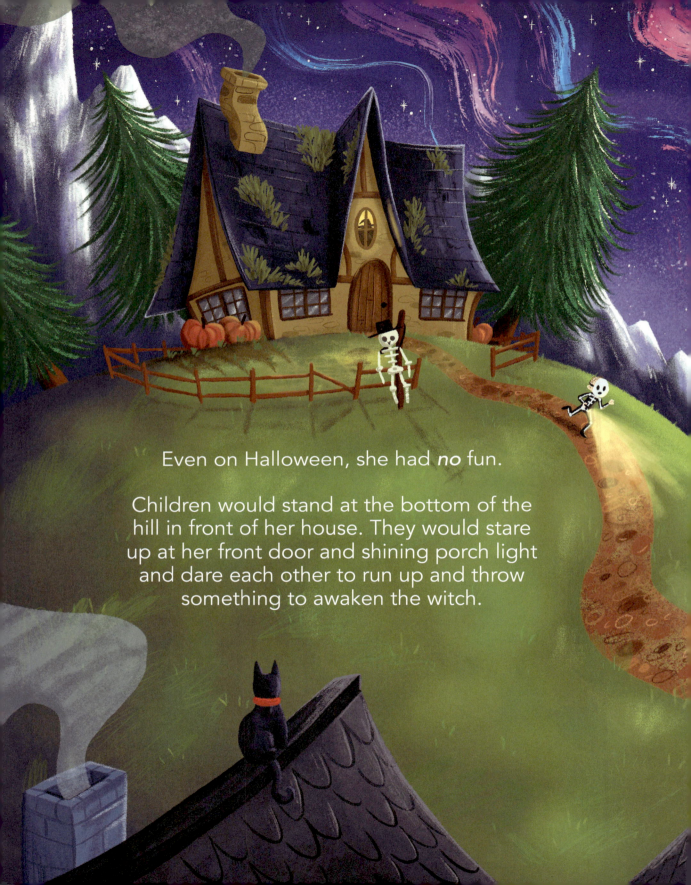

Even on Halloween, she had *no* fun.

Children would stand at the bottom of the hill in front of her house. They would stare up at her front door and shining porch light and dare each other to run up and throw something to awaken the witch.

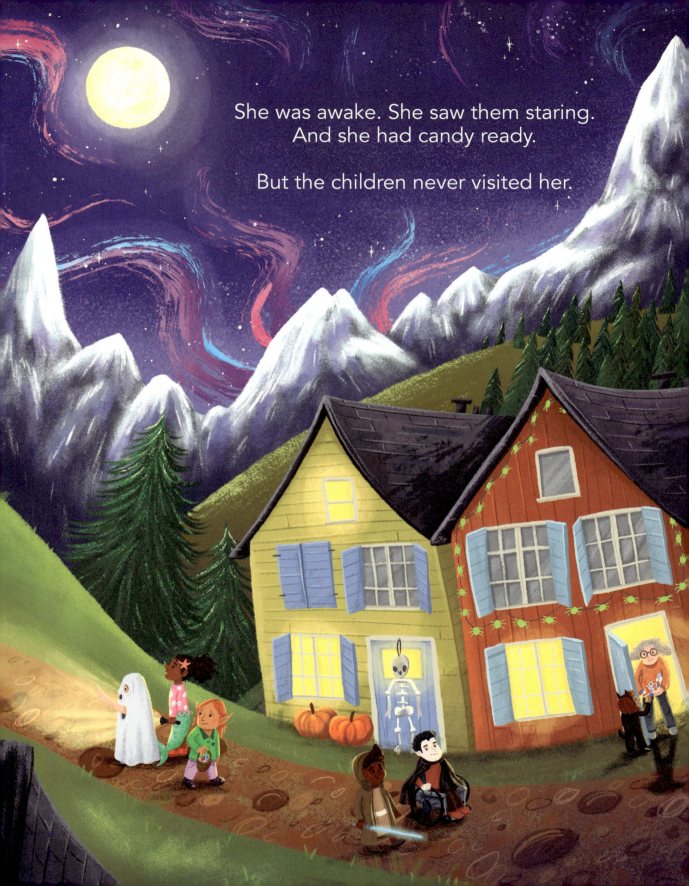

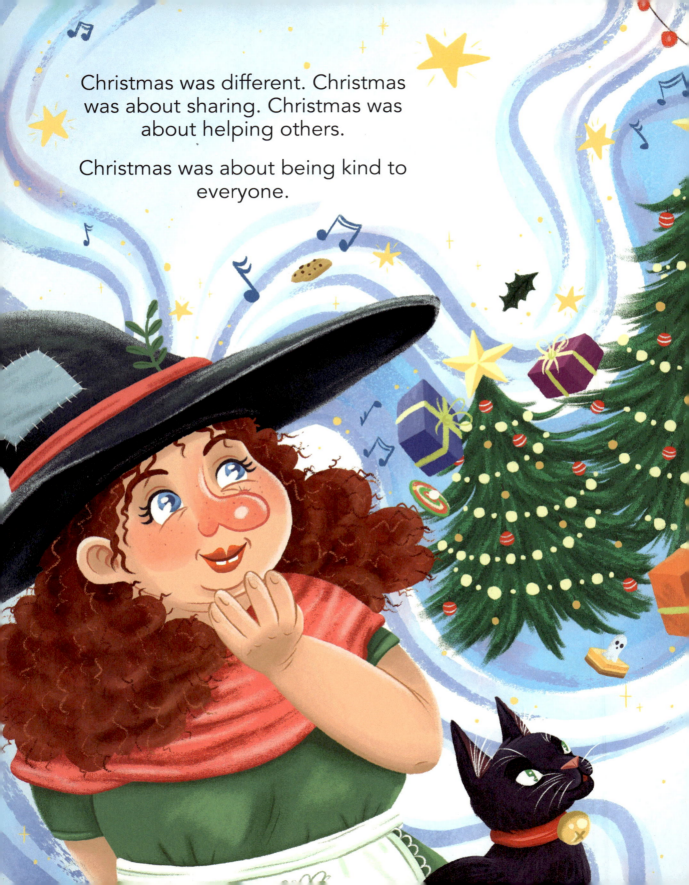

Christmas was different. Christmas was about sharing. Christmas was about helping others.

Christmas was about being kind to everyone.

The witch loved christmas.

She loved the lights on the trees.
She loved the carolers in the streets.
But most of all, she loved the cookies.

This year, for the first time ever, the witch decided to celebrate Christmas too!

She made herself a new bright red dress with a tall green pointed hat.
She put jingle bells on the tips of the curled up pointy toes of her favorite black shoes.

She cut down a tree and decorated it with silvery spider webs and glittery sugar skulls. She stuck a string of green lights around her door with goblin slime.

But most important were the cookies!

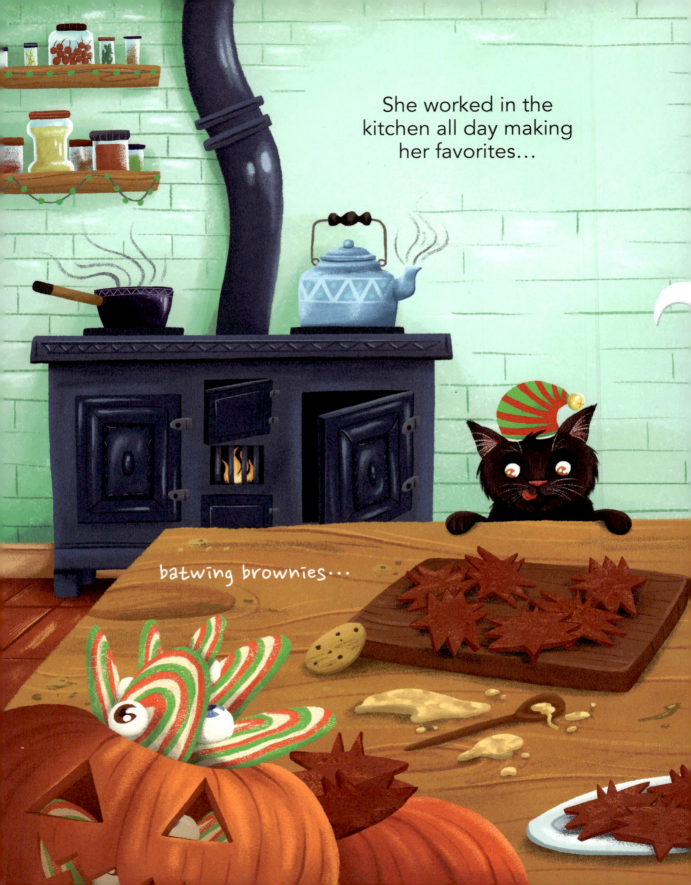

When her work was done, it was almost sunset.
She stood by her front window, behind the spider web curtains, waiting for the villagers to arrive at the town square.

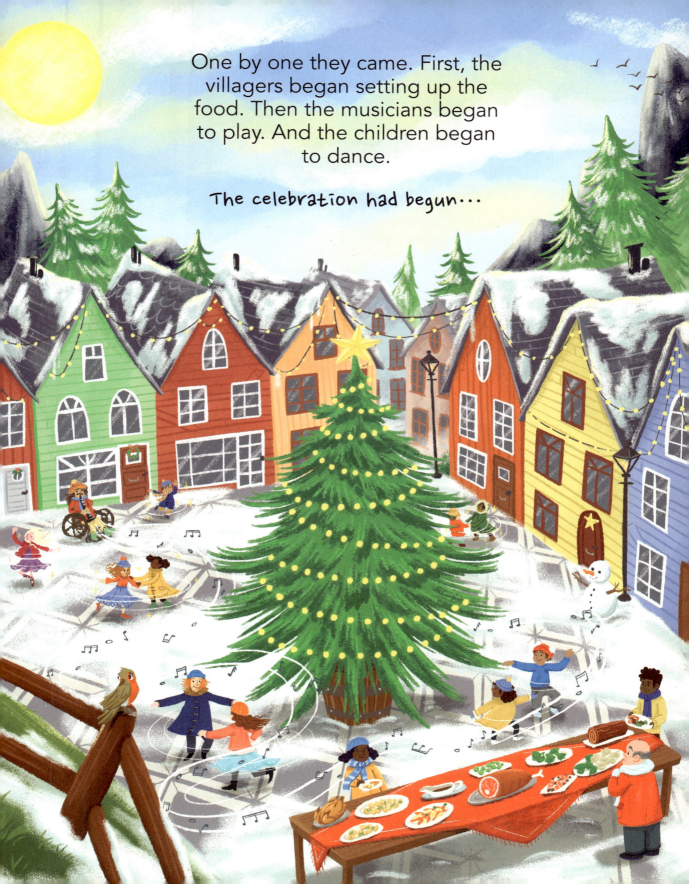

One by one they came. First, the villagers began setting up the food. Then the musicians began to play. And the children began to dance.

The celebration had begun...

Slowly, the witch opened her front door. Carefully, she carried her basket full of cookies down the hill.

She stood at the bottom of the hill, right at the edge of the town square, watching the celebration.

The villagers had not yet noticed her. She could turn around and go home without causing a stir.

But then, someone did notice her bright red dress and pointed at her.
Suddenly, the music stopped...

So scared, the witch froze. She trembled so much that the bells on her curly toe tips jingled quietly. In a very small voice she asked, "Would anyone like to have a cookie?"

The villagers looked confused. The witch had spoken so quietly that no one had heard her.

She took a deep breath, cleared her throat, and spoke as loudly as her scared voice would let her, "Would anyone like to have a cookie?"

*Silence…*

Nobody said a word… until another small voice in the back of the crowd said, "Sure! I'd love to have a cookie."

His name was Louie. And Louie was not afraid. The little boy walked toward the tall witch and looked inside her basket.

These cookies did not look like anything he had *ever* seen before. "What kind are they?" asked Louie.

"Oh!" said the witch in surprise. "I made batwing brownies! And monster lemon bars! And peppermint eyeball pinwheels!"

Louie smiled. "I didn't know that peppermints had eyeballs," he joked. "I'd like a batwing brownie, please."

Was he going to **grow fangs?**

Was he going to **sprout fur?**

Was he going to shrink into a **scaly bug?**

You know what happened?
Louie *smiled*.

The batwing brownie was so good! "Can I have another one?" asked Louie.

"Of course!" replied the witch.

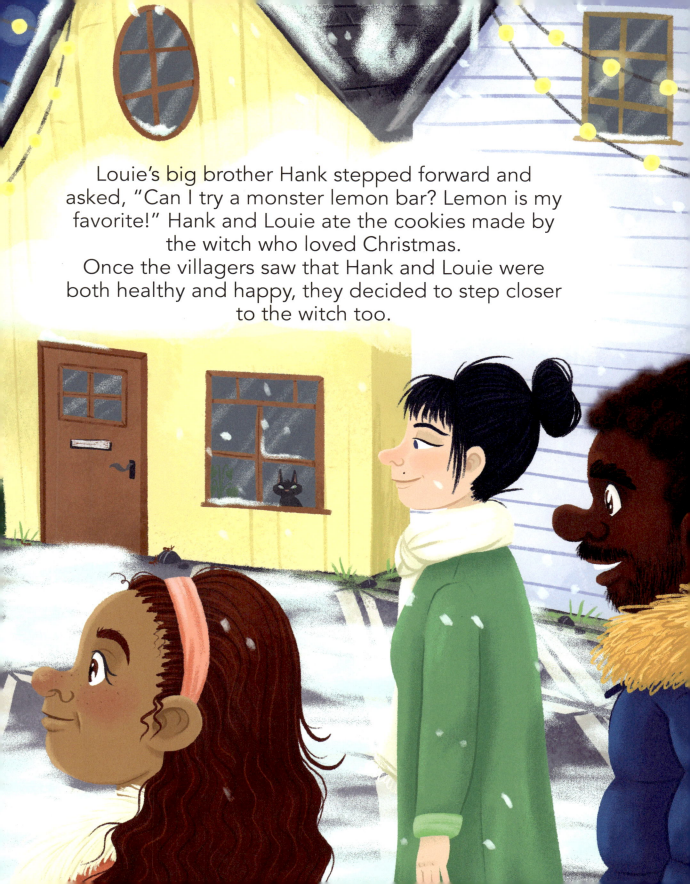

Louie's big brother Hank stepped forward and asked, "Can I try a monster lemon bar? Lemon is my favorite!" Hank and Louie ate the cookies made by the witch who loved Christmas.
Once the villagers saw that Hank and Louie were both healthy and happy, they decided to step closer to the witch too.

One villager brought her a glass of punch.
Another offered her a chair by the band.

Then people invited her to try their cookies
too- and they were *delicious*!
Even without eyeballs.

Soon the musicians began to play again and the celebration continued. The witch clapped her hands to the music, laughed and ate more cookies than she had ever eaten in her whole life.

Finally, the town bells rang. It was time to go to bed before Santa arrived.

The villagers cleaned and packed up and began heading to their homes. The witch began to carry her empty basket back up the hill. But before she could leave, Hank tugged on the witch's new red dress.

"Tomorrow we all have dinner together," said Hank. "You can sit with my family."

The Christmas Witch was so happy!

"Thank you," she said. "I would love to come."

At home, she sipped hot cocoa with whipped slime, sat by her fire and smiled. In the distance she could hear the bells jingle on Santa Claus' sleigh!

This was the *best* Christmas ever...

This book is dedicated to my dad, and his never-ending love of cookies.
~ M.

Copyright © 2021 by Marva Diaz

Illustrations Copyright © 2021 by Lucy Rogers

All rights reserved. This is a work of fiction. The events and characters described here are products of the author's imagination. No part of this book may be used or reproduced in any manner whatsoever without written permission by the publisher, except in the case of brief quotations embodied in critical articles or reviews. For more information, contact Salus Publishing LLC, 5406 Crossings Dr. Ste 102-353, Rocklin, CA 95677.

First edition November 2021.

ISBN (Paperback): 978-1-7335426-3-0

Published by:
Salus Publishing LLC
5406 Crossings Dr.
Ste 102-353
Rocklin, CA 95677

This book is printed on 100% PCW FSC Recycled paper.

We stand with the trees.

www.SalusPublishing.com